FAMOUS FAIRY TALES
COLORING BOOK

MARTY NOBLE

DOVER PUBLICATIONS, INC.
MINEOLA, NEW YORK

Note

Snow White, Sleeping Beauty, Little Tom Thumb, and Jack and the Beanstalk—you'll find these beloved fairy tale characters, and many more, in this delightful coloring book! Add touches of color to pictures of Rapunzel, the Frog Prince, Cinderella, Beauty and the Beast, and Little Red Riding Hood. Delight in thirty enchanting pages of fairy tale adventures as you color scenes from the Brothers Grimm, Hans Christian Andersen, Charles Perrault, Russian and Japanese stories, and others.

Bibliographical Note

Famous Fairy Tales Coloring Book is a new work, first published by Dover Publications, Inc., in 2013.

International Standard Book Number

ISBN-13: 978-0-486-49707-5
ISBN-10: 0-486-49707-0

Manufactured in the United States by RR Donnelley
49707005   2016
www.doverpublications.com

1. Rapunzel

2. Little Red Riding Hood

3. The Princess and the Pea

4. The Emperor's New Clothes

5. Hansel and Gretel

6. Puss in Boots

7. The Little Mermaid

8. Beauty and the Beast

9. Jack and the Beanstalk

10. Bluebeard

11. East of the Sun and West of the Moon

12. The Goose Girl

13. Aladdin and the Wonderful Lamp

14. Cinderella

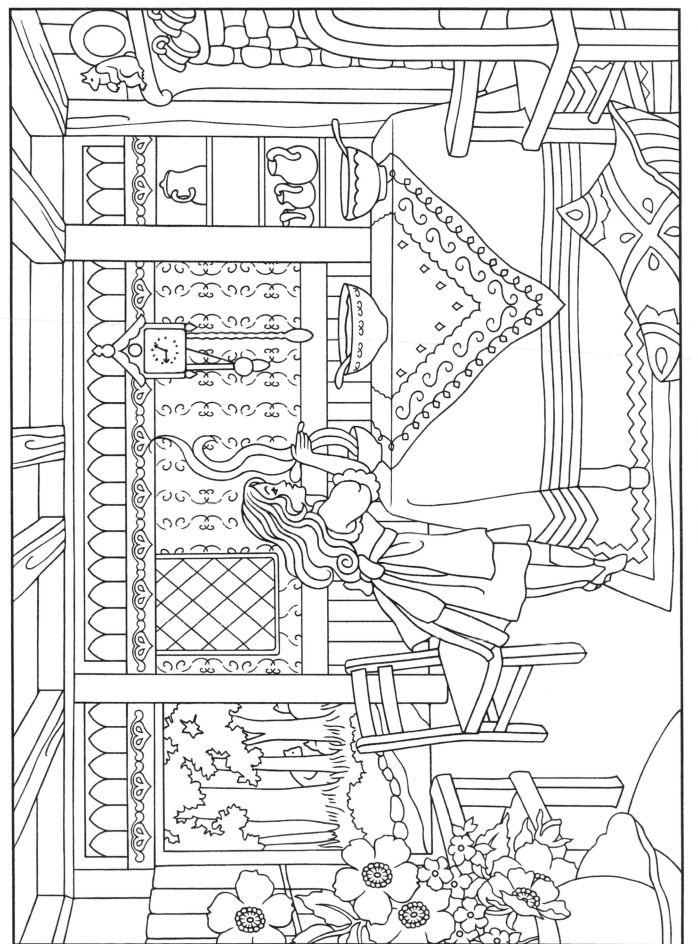

15. Goldilocks and the Three Bears

16. The Fisherman and His Wife

17. Little Tom Thumb

18. The Nightingale

19. Rumpelstiltskin

20. Sleeping Beauty

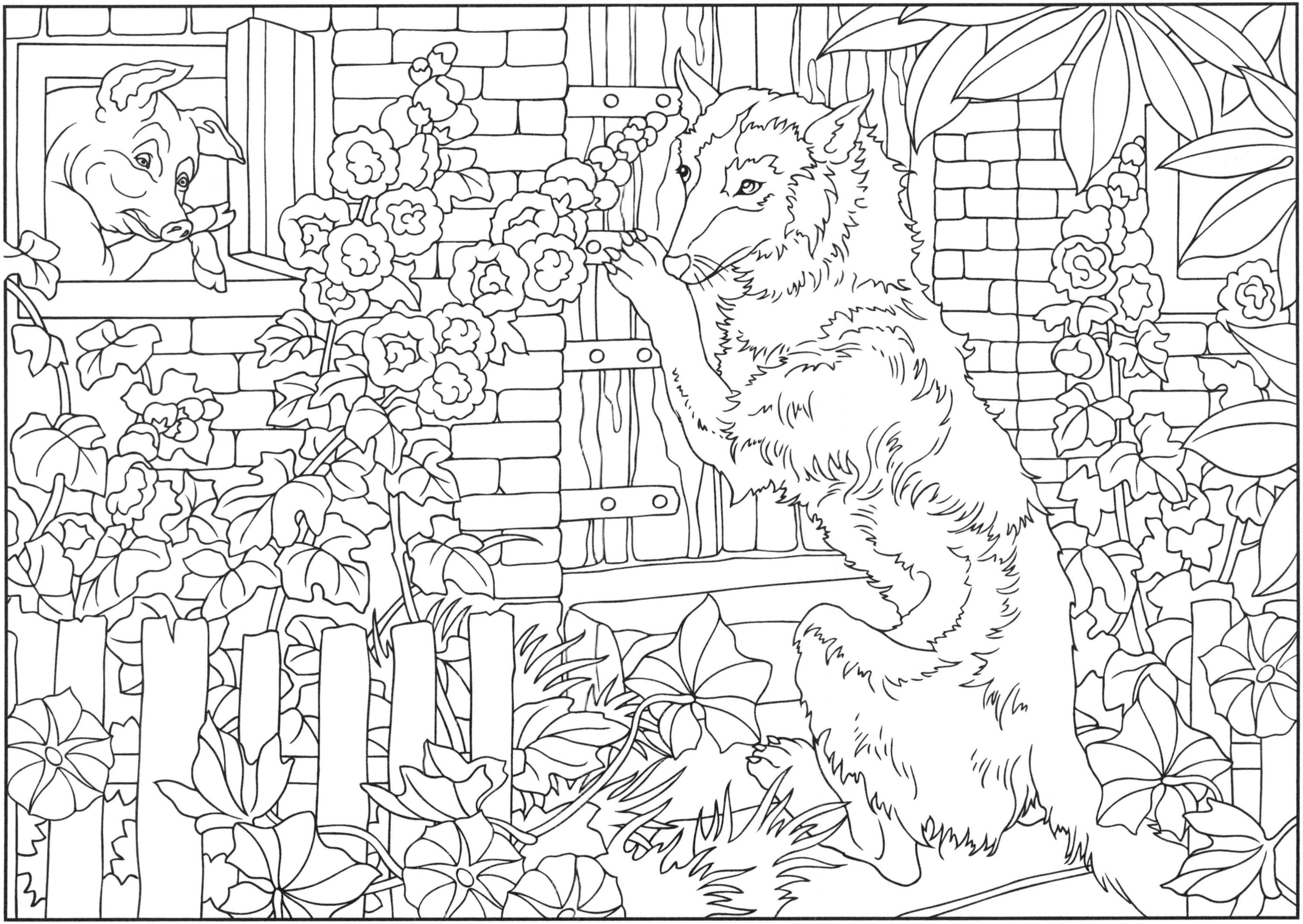
21. The Three Little Pigs

22. Snow White and Rose Red

23. The Frog Prince

24. The Snow Queen

25. The Ugly Duckling

26. Snow White and the Seven Dwarfs

27. The Firebird and Princess Vasilisa

28. The Wild Swans

29. Thumbelina

30. The Twelve Dancing Princesses